FARM EXPLORER

T0081082

Where Do Horses Go When It Rains?

QUESTIONS AND ANSWERS ABOUT FARM BUILDINGS

by Katherine Rawson

CAPSTONE PRESS
a capstone imprint

Published by Pebble Sprout, an imprint of Capstone.
1710 Roe Crest Drive, North Mankato, Minnesota 56003
capstonepub.com

Library of Congress Cataloging-in-Publication Data
Names: Rawson, Katherine, author.
Title: Where do horses go when it rains? : questions and answers about farm buildings / by Katherine Rawson.
Description: North Mankato, Minnesota : Pebble, [2022] | Series: Farm explorer | Audience: Ages 5-8 | Audience: Grades K-1 | Summary: "Barns, silos, sheds, and coops—farms have so many buildings! What are they all for? What animals live in them? Kids can get to know all about the different buildings on farms in this interactive Pebble Sprout series"—Provided by publisher.
Identifiers: LCCN 2021970050 (print) | LCCN 2021058790 (ebook) |
ISBN 9781666349191 (hardcover) | ISBN 9781666349238 (paperback) |
ISBN 9781666349276 (pdf) | ISBN 9781666349351 (kindle edition)
Subjects: LCSH: Farm buildings—Juvenile literature. | Farms—Juvenile literature.
Classification: LCC S782 .R 2022 (print) | LCC S782 (ebook) | DDC 631.2—dc23/eng/20220111
LC record available at https://lccn.loc.gov/2021970050
LC ebook record available at https://lccn.loc.gov/2021970110

Editorial Credits:
Editor: Kristen Mohn; Designer: Sarah Bennett; Media Researcher: Julie De Adder;
Production Specialist: Katy LaVigne

Image Credits:
Alamy: Beth Hall, 12 (bottom); Associated Press: VWPics/Edwin Remsberg, 8 (bottom); Getty Images: amixstudio, 17, deimagine, 16 (top), georgeclerk, 7 (top), GlobalP, 27, nicolesy, 22 (bottom), photograph by dorisj, 25 (bottom right), RonBailey, 3 (top middle), Stefano Oppo, 26, steverts, 3 (middle right); Shutterstock: Abrym, 24, Andrey Kozlovskiy (rain), cover, 14, Anne Richard, 29, Anon Wangkheeree, 28 (top), Charles Brutlag, 3 (bottom left), cherezoff, cover (grass), Colin Woods, 30 (top), Dasha Petrenko, 11 (nursery), David Gaylor, 21 (back), Enrique Alaez Perez, cover (bottom left), Eric Buermeyer, cover (bottom middle), 3 (top left), Eric Isselee, cover (horse), Gelpi, 4, Gus Andi, 9 (chicken), Iakov Kalinin, 15, Ioan Panaite, 9 (tractor), J.T. Images, 5, James Kirkikis, 3 (middle left), jantsarik, 22 (top), Joan Stabnaw, 20, Jolanta Mosakovska, 31 (bottom left), Joy Brown, 6, JungleOutThere, 12 (top), Kenneth Keifer, 31 (top), Lili-OK, 32 (bottom), MaxyM, 3 (bottom right), 19, MotRich-Design, 28 (bottom), Mr Twister, 23 (bottom), Natalie Board, 10, nata-lunata, 32 (top), Olga Pasynkova (background), back cover and throughout, pepsizero, 21 (elevator buttons), Photoagriculture, 18, Rita Kochmarjova, 13, robinimages2013, cover (umbrella), rustycanuck, 14 (back), Sanit Fuangnakhon, 7 (bottom), Santiparp Wattanaporn, 16 (bottom), Scott Prokop, cover (bottom right), SGr, 3 (top right), Sineenuch J, 31 (bottom right), Sophia Carey, 8 (top), Sushaaa, 25 (back), Thodoris Tibilis, 23 (top), Tom Mc Nemar, 3 (middle), Tony Campbell, 11 (baby turkeys), wavebreakmedia, 30 (bottom)

Farmers use all kinds of buildings. They have barns and sheds and coops and more. They need homes for their animals, places to store things, and places to do their work.

Let's find out about different kinds of farm buildings. Read each question and try to guess the answer. Then turn the page to learn the answer.

Did you guess right?

How big is a barn?

There are all kinds of barns, and they come in all sizes. A barn might be just big enough for one horse in a stall, or large enough to hold hundreds of animals!

A barn can be any size the farmer needs it to be.

Where do farmers park their tractors?

Farmers keep their tractors in a large equipment shed with other farm machinery. These are often called machine sheds. The shed also holds spare parts and tools for making repairs.

Do chickens drive chicken tractors?

Chickens don't drive chicken tractors. They live in them!

A chicken tractor is a coop that can be moved around a pasture. That way, the chickens get plenty of bugs and plants to eat. At the same time, they help control pests and weeds around the farm.

Where do baby turkeys live?

Baby turkeys need lots of warmth. In a brooder barn, they get the extra warmth they need, the right kind of food, and plenty of room to grow.

Where do horses go when it rains?

A run-in shed is a shelter for horses in a pasture.
It is open on one side. The horses can go inside
when it's raining, when they need some shade,
or anytime they want.

Where do cows go to get milked?

Cows are milked in a room called a milking parlor. They enter twice a day at milking times. Then, a milking machine is attached to each cow's udder while the cows munch on hay.

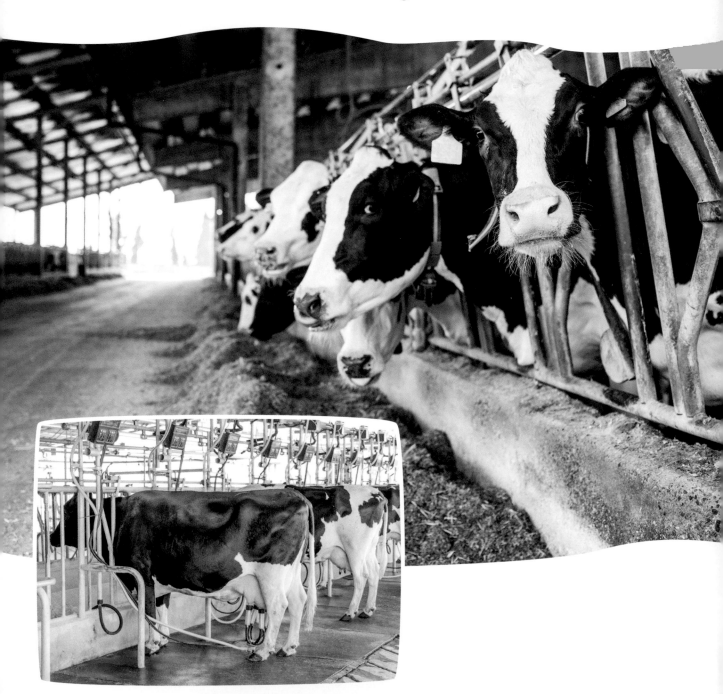

Where does milk go
after it leaves the cow?

The milking machine pumps the milk through pipes to a storage tank in the milk tank room. The tank keeps the milk cool until a truck comes to pick it up.

What's the tallest building on a farm?

If a farm has a silo, that is likely the tallest building. On a dairy farm, a silo holds food called silage for cows. The silage is made of corn or hay. Some silos are more than 100 feet (30 meters) tall. That's a lot of silage!

Is a grain elevator like a people elevator?

Grain elevators are buildings in communities where grains like wheat or corn are grown. They store the grain farmers harvest. Inside the elevator, a machine with buckets lifts the grain up to storage bins.

Later, trucks come to take the grain to market.

Why aren't greenhouses green?

Greenhouses are green—on the inside! The clear glass walls let in plenty of sunlight and trap warmth. This helps the plants inside grow healthy, strong, and green, even when it's cold outside.

What place on a farm
is made just for insects?

HOME
SWEET
HOME

A beehive! A beehive looks like a stack of wooden boxes. Thousands of bees live in each hive. They build their honeycombs on frames inside. Farmers harvest the extra honey when it's ready.

BZZZZZ

That could be a compost shed, which holds piles of manure collected from the animal barns. Stinky! But after the manure has composted, it doesn't stink anymore. It makes excellent fertilizer, which helps crops grow!

What's the sweetest building on a farm?

A sugarhouse is a small building where maple syrup from maple tree sap is made. Inside, a large tank filled with sap sits over a fire. As the sap boils, it turns into sweet maple syrup. Yum!

Fun Farm Facts!

Most barns are shaped like rectangles (4 sides), although you may sometimes see barns that are shaped like hexagons (6 sides), octagons (8 sides), or even shaped like circles.

In a brooder barn, the temperature is turned down a little bit each week. That's because baby chickens and turkeys need less warmth as their feathers grow in. By the time they are 6 or 7 weeks old, they are completely feathered.

How did chicken tractors get their name? Chickens scratch for food in the dirt. This helps loosen the soil, similar to how a tractor pulling a plow would. Chicken droppings also make good fertilizer. A very nice garden can be grown where chickens have been.

One beehive can produce 30, 60, or sometimes even 100 pounds (45 kilograms) of honey in a year. The amount varies depending on weather and other conditions.

In a compost pile, bacteria does the work of turning manure into rich compost. It takes a few months for manure to compost.